© KOM Publishing House 2000

Svein Gran

Vågeveien 10

6509 Kristiansund

Tel.: +47 71 67 83 00

e-mail: komf@online.no

www.kom-forlag.no

Graphic design: Unni Dahl

Repro and printing: PDC Tangen AS

Other photographers:

Page 23: Kristiansund, photo: Odd Holm

Molde, photo: Svein Roger Ivarsen

ISBN 82 90823 60 6

Cover: Blomberg, an abandoned farm overlooking the Geirangerfjord.
Inside front cover: A rock sculpted by aeons of storms and ice, at Torskangerpollen on the island of Vågsøy.
Title page: The Geirangerfjord with the silhouette of Pulpit Rock on the left and Seven Sisters falls in the distant background.

Fjord Norway

author
Olav Grinde

photographer
Per Eide

KOM FORLAG

Contents

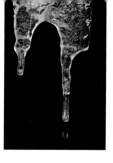

The Story of Water

Each day the sun climbs higher above the horizon. Gradually, cold winter nights turn brighter. Ice and snow retreat from the dawning rays of sun, minutely lessening the snowcaps on mountains.

Drip drop of melting snow, trickling over the stones into a tiny beck. Rivers form. They break up the ice that has covered them, rush over clifftops, thundering against rocks hundreds of meters below – this is the farewell song of winter. Quietly, the crystal clear waters reunite, stretch their arms and follow their ancient paths toward the sea. Some of them are canyons dug deep through aeons.

The story of Norway is inseparable from the story of water. Before history was written, wanderers settled our coasts and found havens where the ice had retreated. With care and fear they harvested the sea, hunted the fields and forests. Then the Vikings mastered the waters. They built strong vessels and the wind carried them to faraway lands. They grabbed their oars and rowed far upstream on foreign rivers. By the mouth of one of them, they built Dublin.

You have to know the bleakness of winter, see it bleach the colours from the landscape, covering its hues in a mantle of white. Only then can you truly enjoy spring! Fjord Norway has few visitors during that time of year, when colours emerge from their hidden places. From one day to the next, the landscape seems renewed in delicate shades and vibrant hues. Moisture is drawn up into swelling buds, soft green leaves, unfolding flowers.

It's no secret that it rains in Fjord Norway. But when the sun breaks the cloud-cover again, and every leaf and stone and blade of grass are moist, the lush landscape seems like a million-faceted emerald.

In the sun's warm rays, children hurry to slurp in their ice cream before it melts into a white trickle. But up above, the glittering ice of the glacier retains its frozen heart. There, you can go skiing even on the hottest day in July.

Glaciers do melt, of course, releasing drops that may have been bound in ice for five thousand years. That's the best drinking water anywhere. Just bend down and dip your cupped hand into the ice cold glacier river – or buy it bottled at the local store.

Salmon rush up the rivers, even traversing waterfalls before they can mate! Kings and lords have been joined by many less noble, if no less enthusiastic fishermen. Beneath drizzle or sun, the fly fisherman seems immersed in his own world, trying to read the river and outsmart the fish.

The mild winds and long, warm days of late summer dry out the land. Then the vibrant colours of autumn are lit. A new wind comes, less patient, whipping the coastal waters to a foaming frenzy. High waves pound the rocks, again and again. The sea throws driftwood high up on the shores and sprays its salty water onto the fields beyond; even the inland valleys quiver. But the innermost fjords remain calm and boats and gulls retreat here until the storm blows over. On a day without wind, the mirroring fjord matches the splendour of the skies. Sometimes the drizzle makes scarcely a sound. Then the hard wind returns with drenching autumn rains and hail to rip the leaves from the trees.

Suddenly one day there's frost on the ground. The tourists are gone and the birds have flown south. Distances seem to increase even though we know that's illusion.

But before the land submits to its icy sleep, before the first silent snow falls, before the sun's reflection glows one last time in the ice which creeps over the thousand lakes, and the long, drawn-out night throws its cloak of darkness over northern parts – the new spring has already sown its seeds. And these tiny seeds lie patiently under the snow, waiting. And so do we. We wait for the sun to rise once again above the horizon, wait for the sun's rays to warm the snow – for the first drip drop of melting ice.

The Fjord – the Soul of Western Norway

Hardangerfjord –
Apple Blossoms
Beneath the
Glacier

*The fields haven't been completely
cleared of stones! Below Vefoss in
Sandvedalen.*

*Top right: Many children in
Hardanger know of trails leading
to a private haven.*

No time in Hardanger is more magical than when the apple blossoms unfold at the end of May. The fruit orchards along the fjord seem to consist entirely of pale flowers, which compete in glory with the dazzling glacier and snow-topped mountains above. It is said that the first apple seeds were planted by Cistercian monks from Lysekloster monastery outside Bergen, who owned a farm at Opedal.

Even after the flower petals have fallen, the Hardangerfjord is a feast for the eye, especially the lush northwestern shore, where the calcareous bedrock has yielded fertile soil. Between the fruit orchards are groves and woods of warmth-loving trees such as alder and linden, oak and ash, hazel and maple. Five thousand years ago, when the climate was even milder, there were great forests of such trees in Norway.

Farmhouses and boathouses roofed with Hardanger slate blend beautifully into the fertile cultural landscape lining the fjord. Even when old walls give way, the roofs may be intact and they seem indestructible.

Innermost in one of the fjord arms lies the picturesque village of Ulvik. One of Norway's finest 20th century poets, Olav H. Hauge, was an apple farmer here. As you sail into the fjord and fjord arms, you pass many villages. It's hard to pick out just one to visit; they all have their own charm – Utne and Eidfjord, Strandebarm and Norheimsund, to mention a few!

Viewing the Barony in Rosendal for the first time is like rediscovering a wonderful old memory. Just as impressive are the Renaissance gardens which are used for concerts and historical plays.

One of the most striking waterfalls in all of Norway is Vøringsfossen, with a free fall of 182 metres into the abyss of Måbødalen. The water throws itself over the precipice and seems suspended for a few glorious seconds. The road takes its time, slowly winding vehicles down into the valley below. The oldest road in Måbødalen, however, is no more than a footpath, with 124 turns and 1300 patiently restored steps ascending the mountainside.

At the end of the 19th century, Odda was the most popular cruising destination in Norway. For thousands of tourists, the great attraction was Tyssestrengene falls in nearby Tyssedalen, then the third highest falls in Europe. But when engineer Sam Eyde viewed the falls in 1906 he had a different vision, a vision of man taming these raging forces of nature and exploiting them in the service of a new prosperity. A few years later there was a power station here and industry was established on the shores of the fjord at Odda. The dramatic history of the early industrial pioneers is told at the industrial museum in Tyssedal.

For many centuries, the rich forests of Hardanger provided timber for Scotland and England, as well as materials for the many boatyards in Hardanger. The region has maintained its old boat-building traditions. At Norheimsund, there is a boat-building museum which has restored many vessels. The first was S/J Mathilde, a Hardanger sloop which is now a windborne museum travelling the coast of western Norway. The oldest boat built of planks found in Norway, on Halsnøy at the mouth of the fjord, was built in approx. 330 AD.

Do you hear music? It may not just be birdsong. Perhaps an aspiring young musician is playing the double-stringed Hardanger fiddle, the main instrument of Norwegian folk music. One of the best instrument-makers works at the Hardanger

Folk Museum, a cultural oasis in Utne.
Should you be lucky enough to see a
traditional wedding, be sure to study
the details of the colourful costumes.
A Hardanger bride is a fairytale princess
– when she weds, she even wears a silver
crown!

*In 1794, a priest in Hardanger published a book
admonishing everyone to use slate – a gift of God,
a wonderful resource, and a fabulous building
material. Today, many buildings with slate roofs
lining the fjord arms and sounds of the famous
fjord. Here, the sound near Børsheimholmen.*

Sognefjord – the Longest Fjord

A river empties its waters into the Aurlandsfjord, near Beitelen.

If the Sognefjord were drained of water, and you stood at its deepest point, you would find yourself 1308 metres below sea level peering up at mountains more than three kilometres high! Travellers from abroad have appreciated the scenery along Norway's longest fjord since long before the heyday of modern tourism in the middle of the 19th century.

When World War I broke out, Kaiser Wilhelm II of Germany was on holiday in the village of Balestrand, visiting his friend, the painter Hans Dahl. Norwegian authorities gave the Kaiser an ultimatum to leave Norwegian territory by 6 pm that very day. Not being a man to have his pleasures cut short, Kaiser Wilhelm took his jolly good time drinking his tea, enjoying conversation with his host and savouring impressions of the surrounding landscape – before heading full steam out the fjord aboard his yacht, minutes before the deadline expired!

Balestrand, a place once favoured by artists, is known for its many ornate Swiss-style houses. It's just one of many charming and eye-catching villages along the 205 km long Sognefjord. Between the villages are healthy green forests, farms with rolling lush pastures, and screes where mountains have sent rocks tumbling toward the fjord.

The scenery is especially dramatic at Beitelen, where the famous Nærøyfjord branches off from the Aurlandsfjord. There is still an old wooden quay where farmers would disembark with their sheep and head for greener grazing land in the mountains above.

For many cruise passengers, the Nærøyfjord is the climax of western Norway. There is a real danger of getting a stiff neck from peering up toward the tops of 1200 metre high mountains along the narrowing fjord. At Styve it's only a few hundred metres across, and near the idyllic village of Bakka, it's not much wider. The road from Gudvangen, at the bottom of the fjord, turns into a series of hairpin bends at Stalheimskleiva. Near the hotel at the top, there is a private folk museum.

The Aurlandsfjord proper continues to Aurland and Flåm. Many fishermen have wonderful memories of salmon caught in the Aurland river – and they're not tall tales! You too will have a good story to tell after taking the train from Flåm to Myrdal, or vice versa; railway buffs consider Flåmsbana one of the most exciting

The Nærøyfjord is perhaps the most scenic and famous of the many arms of the Sognefjord.

Top: Contrary to popular belief, the Sognefjord is not the longest fjord in the world. The Nordvest-fjord in Greenland is half again as long, but it is covered with ice most of the year and no one lives along its shores.

train rides in all of Europe. The 20 km long railway, which passes through 20 tunnels, took 20 years to build.

At the Sogn Folk Museum, situated between Sogndal and Kaupanger, you can study 35 buildings collected from the fjord districts, some of them 500 years old, and more than 20 000 objects.

If you are looking for a fine old Norwegian book, you stand a good chance of finding a real bargain, and perhaps even a first edition of the title you want in Fjærland. Hordes of book lovers from all over Norway descend on the village during the summer months. Amongst travellers, however, Fjærland is better known as the home of the Norwegian Glacier Museum. It's a perfect place to learn about the inner life of the nearby Jostedalsbreen glacier, before accompanying an experienced guide for a walk on the glacier itself.

At the end of one of the innermost arms of the Sognefjord lies the best preserved village in all of Sogn and Fjordane county – Lærdalsøyri. One of Norway's most famous salmon rivers flows right through the centre of town. The oldest houses here date from the late 18th century.

Four of Norway's stave churches stand on the shores of the Sognefjord, while a fifth, Borgund, stands 27 km inland from Lærdalsøyri. The most famous of them all, and the oldest, is Urnes. The surrounding landscape on the promontory where it stands overlooking the Lustrafjord has not changed much since it was built around 1150. Both Borgund and Hopperstad have almost a fairytale appearance and are beautifully preserved, while you may drive past Undredal without ever realising it's a stave church. Kaupanger, too, has seen many changes in the course of centuries.

Modern engineers have drilled holes through many mountains in western Norway, even under the glacier, and have bridged many islands and fjords. But if you have to cross the Sognefjord, and want to avoid taking a ferry, you still have to drive halfway to the Swedish border.

The Varied Landscape of Nordfjord

Tranquil waters in Stryn.

The autumn and spring storms that sweep against the Norwegian coastline have Stad as their favourite meeting place. This desolate landscape, virtually devoid of trees, has a stark beauty. In the tall coastal cliffs, the relentless onslaught of the sea has carved caves both above and below the waterline. There are more shipwrecks on the sea floor here than anywhere else along the coast. In Ervik, a cemetery commemorates one of the great tragedies of World War II; 44 Norwegians and an unknown number of German soldiers were killed when allied bombers sunk the coastal steamer, St. Svithun.

Long before roads gained their modern prominence, Selje was the most important harbour between Bergen and Trondheim. The Vikings sometimes sought shelter on this island to sit out storms which could rage for weeks. However, not everyone was patient enough to wait; some actually pulled their boats across the peninsula of Stadlandet at Dragseidet, despite a distance of 5 km and a strenuous climb up to 240 metres!

A thousand years ago, Benedictine monks from England founded a monastery on the island of Selje. It was built below the cave where the body of St. Sunniva was found, supposedly as fresh and intact as if she were sleeping; according to legend, the Irish princess stranded here after she had to flee Ireland in order to avoid being married to a heathen king against her will.

The ruins of monasteries seem to disappear faster than the wear of time would account for. It was quite common for farmers to acquire at least one stone from a holy monastery and incorporate it into the foundation of their houses, so that both dwellings and families would be blessed by the Lord.

Southeast of Selje, near the mouth of the Nordfjord, lies Måløy, one of the most important fishing communities in western Norway. The old lighthouse on the island's northern tip, Kråkenes, stands in a stunning setting. At Vingen, on the

Peering down on the ruins of Selje monastery, from the cave where the intact remains of Saint Sunniva were found.

southern shore of the fjord mouth, there are more petroglyphs than anywhere else in northern Europe. Just across the sound are the magnificent sea cliffs of Hornelen.

From here, the Nordfjord cuts inland, eventually branching out into a number of arms. The landscape of Nordfjord is softer than the more famous Geirangerfjord and the Sognefjord, with a lush cultural landscape and rounded mountains and hills lining the fjord.

The lakes and deep inland valleys are more dramatic; in some of them, the glacier arms of Jostedalsbreen have been making marked advances in recent years. Precipitous cliffs surround Lake Loenvatnet. The waves on lakes usually don't amount to much, but on 13 September 1936, a huge section of Ramnefjell broke loose and fell into the lake. It raised a flood wave that swept a sightseeing boat deep into the forest. Fortunately, no one was onboard for the ride!

Don't count on sinking your fishing line to the bottom of Lake Hornindal — at 514 metres, it is the deepest in Europe. On the eastern shore is a museum dedicated to Anders Svor, a fine figurative sculptor.

There is no reason to let the season stop you if you want to go skiing or snowboarding; near the county border, not far from Videseter viewpoint, there is a summer ski centre. The adventurous may spend a week crossing the glacier on skis, not necessarily seeking the shortest route.

In their own humble way, Norwegians are fond of taking credit for great events. Some historians have claimed, in all seriousness, that Christopher Columbus was actually from Nordfjord, from a farming family in Hyen.

Top:
The rugged cliffs and mountains of Vågsøy. The mouth of the Nordfjord is seen at the far right.

Top: Veteran trains still occasionally traffic the Rauma railway.

The hairpin turns of Trollstigen were quite an engineering feat when they were completed in 1936.

The Geirangerfjord with Gjerdefossen falls in the foreground.

The famous Geirangerfjord does not start at the sea. It is really an arm of a greater fjord system. The Storfjord (which actually means "the great fjord") starts south of Ålesund and gradually narrows as it winds its way inland, the mountains on both sides rising ever higher. A bit past the village of Stranda, it splits into the Norddalsfjord and the Synnylvsfjord – and it is from this latter fjord that the Geirangerfjord branches off.

A group of enthusiasts are restoring and maintaining a number of deserted farms perched on mountain ledges along the fjord, such as Knivsflå. The roaring waterfalls known as the Seven Sisters, only a couple of hundred metres away, certainly make themselves heard here. Across the fjord lies the farm of Skageflå. In days of old, young men and women supposedly courted by calling out to each other; that is a far cry from being able to whisper sweet things in the ear of your beloved!

There's a story about how Friaren became a bottle-shaped waterfall. The Suitor, as the fall may be called in English, proposed to each of the Seven Sisters. After being turned down by all of them, he was heartbroken and drowned his sorrows in drink – hence the bottle.

These waterfalls did not always look so impressive. In the 1930s, Ole Knivsflå took it upon himself to clean up and divide the watercourse feeding the waterfall, splitting it more clearly into seven separate falls. His motive: to create a more memorable tourist attraction!

The fertile land on these mountain shelves provided these farming families with virtually everything they needed. A few cows, goats and sheep supplied milk and butter, meat and cheese, wool and leather. Grass and leaves had to be cut to feed the animals over the long winter. Potatoes and vegetables were grown in a small patch near the house. More than one visitor, however, has left these farms wondering how these farmers ever managed to install the tether line which was used for bringing other supplies up from the fjord.

A recent American tenant found that conditions were ideal for apricots, but when he also started growing illegal herbs, he was quickly deported!

Innermost in the fjord lies the village of Geiranger. Only 300 people live here year-round. In the winter months, it is not uncommon for them to be isolated when snow slides block the road across the mountains. In the summer, however, population figures may exceed 5000, as tourists arrive by tour bus and car, cruise ship, or ferry from Hellesylt.

From the top of Mount Dalsnibba, 1495 m, there is a fantastic view over the fjord. There is also a dramatic view from Flydalsjuvet, a stone tongue which juts out high above a river canyon, not far from the old Hotel Bellevue.

Those arriving by sea should allow time for onshore excursions. The so-called Golden Route continues by road up to Ørnesvingen viewpoint, with its magnificent panorama, before slowly descending toward the ferry quay at Eidsdal. On the other side of the Norddalsfjord lies Valldal, known for providing the juiciest, tastiest strawberries in the whole region!

Before you approach the valley of Isterdalen, you see the towering peaks known as the Bishop, the King and the Queen. They can be climbed, but only by ramblers unafraid of peering into the abyss; this is not the place to miss a step. The tempting

Trollstigen trail leads to Trolltindene, the pinnacles perched above the mountain wall known to every rock climber in the world – Trollveggen.

Of course you don't have to continue by foot. The road down Isterdalen leads to the town of Åndalsnes, the gateway to further adventures.

Top:
Sure beats our view at home, doesn't it!
The deserted farm at Blomberg.

Trollveggen, one of the most formidable climbs in the world, glows after the morning fog dissipates.

Facing the Sea

Bulandet, the westernmost community in Norway. There are 365 islands, one for every day of the year.

The local store in Sogndalsstrand has been lovingly restored.

From Veidholmen, the northernmost fishing village in Fjord Norway.

The coastal sea route was the main thoroughfare in all but modern times. Whereas on land there are traces of old roads and thoroughfares dating back to Viking times, the wake of a boat leaves no trace. Instead, there are ancient harbours and old fishing villages, trading posts and old inns, the occasional written account and the evidence of place names.

Fishing villages were established so that fishermen could be as close as possible to the fishing grounds, not least of all during the rich herring fisheries of the 19th century. When engines increased the reach of vessels, the most remote and exposed villages were gradually abandoned as people moved onto the mainland or to more sheltered areas. Some of the settlements that once teemed with the activity of thousands of fishermen have found new means to make a livelihood, while others today seem to be permanently asleep.

Some of these beautifully situated villages, however, have received positive attention and attentive care in the last decade. Gradually the houses have been refurbished, and it's not uncommon for Norwegian families or appreciative foreign tourists to rent them for a week or three.

There are many treasures – Espevær, Sogndalsstrand in the south, Krosshamn, Glesvær, Kræmmerholmen and Fedje, Utvær, Bulandet, Bud, Grip and Veidholmen. And that is only mentioning a few.

All but a minuscule portion of Norway's gross national product is produced within a few kilometres of the coast or on the oil platforms offshore. That is why most of the villages and towns of the four counties of Fjord Norway still overlook the sea or fjord.

A fisherman returns with his early morning catch to the southwestern village of Sogndalsstrand.

Jæren and Southwestern Norway

Rock fences divide the cultivated expanses of Jæren, with Kvassheim lighthouse in the distance.

Back from an outing, the family boat returns to the harbour of Egersund.

According to one 16th century priest, the landscape south of Jæren was formed "by the wrath of God".

The sky above Jæren somehow seems different from that of the rest of western Norway. Many Norwegian artists have been inspired by the light here, amongst them Kitty Kielland, Eilif Peterssen, Fritz Thaulow and Harriet Backer. Others who come here, too, are invariably fascinated by the endless beaches, and the wide expanses of cultural landscape interrupted only by rock fences, scattered trees or spread out farmhouses. The breeze makes billowing patterns in the grain fields, as though golden velvet were being caressed by divine hands.

The open landscape of Jæren, along the coast south of Stavanger, was one of the first areas freed of ice over 14 000 years ago, when the recent Ice Age started to relax its cold grip. When the first hunters arrived 8000 years ago, there were forests many places where there is now farmland. At Ullandhaug, an ancient farm has been reconstructed by the Stavanger Museum of Archaeology; a fascinating aspect of the project is that the farm is populated with volunteers who show how life was lived in the early Iron Age.

The surf of the restless sea washes away footprints and worries of countless wanderers. Orresanden, all of 5 km long, is the longest sandy beach in Norway. The slowly shifting sand of Jæren would advance like an encroaching sea were it not for the farmers, who more than a hundred years ago planted marram grass to bind the sand dunes and protect their crops.

When dark, moist earth is upturned by plows, hungry birds have a feast. Before the farmers of Jæren drained many lakes and wetlands in the latter part of the 19th century, bird life here was even richer.

At Jæren, the wind rarely rests even between the highest sand dunes. The wind harp, which accompanied the penetrating sound of Jan Garbarek's saxophone on his record "Dis", was recorded here.

Near Ogna, further south, the landscape changes. Sandy beaches give way to an uneven, stony landscape. The road is no longer straight, the curves force you to slow down. Not everyone has been able to see the stark beauty of this barren landscape. The 16th century priest and

It's rare indeed that raindrops fall on the roofs of these farm houses at Helleren!

The farmers of Jæren have to build their boathouses some distance from the pounding surf.

saga translator, Peder Claussøn Friis, called it "the landscape formed by the wrath of God".

North of Egersund is the huge St. Olav's Serpent, a winding 500 m moraine that looks more like a huge landscape sculpture. Egersund is the largest fisheries port in the country, at least measured on the basis of catches landed. On the island that shields the town, Eigerøya, stands one of the most powerful lighthouses in northern Europe.

Do watch the road as you follow the hairpin turns down to the Jøssingfjord – there is not much to protect you from the abyss below. Few Norwegian cabins or houses have seen less rain than those huddled under the protective stone overhang of Helleren. Grateful tenants have lived here from the Stone Age until the place was abandoned in the 1930s.

We'll be honest; the North Sea Highway is not the fastest link between Fjord Norway and Norway's southern coast. But unlike those who travel the inland route of E39, you will arrive invigorated by a fantastic and varied coastal drama.

Three Towns Built on Herring

Skudeneshavn is perhaps the most well-kept town in Fjord Norway. Believe it or not, this is the main street in the old section of town!

Right page: Most things you needed could be had at the local store.

The galleon figure gazes out over the harbour of Skudeneshavn and back to bygone days. The sailing ships which carried herring to faraway countries are all gone, but this charming, little wooden town still maintains a harmonious character.

There are over 125 traditional, old wooden buildings and 100 boathouses in the well-kept fishing village on the southern tip of the island of Karmøy, sheltered by small island. It was founded during the rich herring fishing periods of the 19th century. At its most prosperous time, the locals took over most of the trade from the rich tradesmen in Bergen and Stavanger. They fished and salted their own produce, and exported it abroad on their own sailing ships. The town had an impressive fleet of trading vessels, especially compared with the number of inhabitants.

Skudeneshavn has grown in an "organic" fashion. When new Norwegian building regulations went into effect in 1854, they were simply ignored by the authorities of Skudeneshavn who claimed that the cliffs and islets "... are obstacles to compliance with the regulations."

The main road winds its way, almost path-like, between the white, wooden buildings – no chess-board blocks of streets here. The narrow space between the cliffs and the sea has been cleverly utilised, but there is hardly room for new buildings.

While Stavanger was founded as early as 1125, the population did not really grow until the 19th century – once again thanks to the rich herring fisheries. The most fascinating part of the town is Old Stavanger, one of the largest concentrations of wooden buildings in Northern Europe. The old workers homes, which huddle together along narrow, cobblestone streets, are almost invariably white. This is not a museum; the residents are grateful locals who know how to appreciate the charm of

The harbour in Haugesund still teems with life.

Left: Elsewhere it might be a museum. Old Stavanger is a living residential community with a charm all its own.

this little town, in the midst of the city which is the oil and gas capital of Norway.

The town of Haugesund would not have existed as such if it had not been for the dramatically prosperous herring fisheries. As recently as 1801 there were a mere 15 souls residing along the sound; in 1845 there were 149 people here, but by 1855 the population had exploded to 1066. Haugesund can rightly be said to have been "built on herring bones".

When the fisheries declined, Haugesund had already established itself as a shipping capital, with a fleet of ships sailing the seven seas.

What do you do with a newly gained fortune? You build a castle to impress your neighbour! A good example of how much this meant is the Knutsen villa. The mansion was originally designed in the Nordic baroque style in 1895. When a nearby farmer, who made his own fortune by salting great quantities of herring, built a true copy, the shipping magnate immediately issued orders that his own house was to be rebuilt!

Unlike most Norwegian towns, there has been no large-scale fire to clean up the town of Haugesund. As a result, it is a study in the contrast of styles, ranging from Art Nouveau and classicism to the misproportioned concrete monstrosities built in the 1970s. Many of the older houses on street corners are equipped with fancy towers – so much so that Haugesund has been called "the town of towers".

Bergen, the City of Seven Mountains

For nearly a thousand years travellers by sea have been welcomed by the many moods of Bergen's harbour.

Rome may be built on seven hills, but only Bergen has the distinction of being wreathed by seven mountains. When the sun breaks through the cloud cover, Bergeners forget that it may have rained for days on end. For summer visitors, the weather gods seem to clear the sky of clouds.

To walk amongst the centuries' old buildings of Bryggen is to travel back in time to the days when the export of dried fish brought great prosperity to Bergen – or rather to the Hanseatic tradesmen who governed this wharf and the nearby harbour. They even held services in German in their own church, dedicated to the Virgin Mary, the oldest in Bergen. Archaeological finds at the nearby Bryggen Museum indicate that Bryggen has been a centre of business since before the city was founded in 1070. Today, the 58 well-kept buildings are occupied by craftsmen and workshops, restaurants and stores.

A couple of minutes' walk away is Håkonshallen, a Mediaeval stone hall where kings once ruled. It was carefully restored after a powerful explosion on Hitler's birthday in 1944, aboard a munitions ship which the German occupants had docked at a nearby quay.

There is far more wooden architecture worth seeing. Over the last two decades,

You may be astonished at how many languages the fish mongers master at Bergen's famous fish market!

hundreds of old wooden houses in the Sandviken and Nordnes areas have been lovingly restored. In some ways, these living neighbourhoods are even more impressive than Old Bergen museum, the carefully arrayed collection of buildings situated north of the town centre.

For art lovers, there is also an enviable concentration of museums around the central lake.

One of the most impressive houses in all of Bergen is Damsgård Manor, built in the 18th century. Of more humble size but with just as grand a view is Troldhaugen, 10 km south of Bergen, where composer Edvard Grieg and his wife Nina lived when they were not travelling the continent on concert tours. Another composer, Harald Sæverud, also built a distinguished home – Siljustøl.

Bergen is sometimes referred to as "Norway's secret capital". For centuries it has been the most cultural and international city in the country. There are many reasons why Bergen was selected as a European City of Culture for the year 2000. For years, stoneworkers have been busy repaving many alleys and streets with cobblestones.

You may notice tens of thousands of rhododendron blossoming along the thoroughfares of Bergen. Most were donated by a native son, a businessman who wanted to share his riches with the town. In the 19th century, other town patriots established Fjellveien (the mountain road), a fine promenade that you can stroll along at your own pace and absorb the impressions of the historic town below.

No visit to Bergen is complete without a bird's eye view. The Fløibanen funicular brings you up to a wonderful view of Bergen. Many people appreciate long walks in these mountains. Mount Ulriken, the highest of Bergen's seven mountains, undoubtedly offers the most magnificent panorama of the region.

If you see a traffic jam, it may not necessarily be due to rush hour. Should you hear drumming, then it's almost certainly one of the "buekorps" marching, uniformed boys' corps complete with bayonets and make-believe crossbows. Where else in the world can bands of juvenile boys march in the middle of the street, obviously taking their time, despite impatient drivers, without endangering their lives and health? Lord have mercy on the foreigner (especially one from Oslo) who writes a letter to the local newspaper editor complaining about this colourful Bergen tradition!

A Sunday view from Fløyen.

Bryggen and the Hanseatic Tradesmen

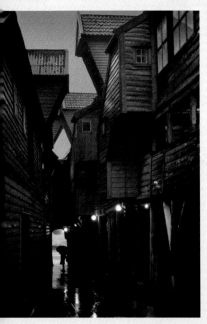

The distinctive row of gable-end buildings glows in the evening sun, warming proud Bergeners as well as inquisitive tourists. We won't mention names, but the surviving politicians and businessmen who decades ago lobbied hardest to have the dilapidated Bryggen torn down are now embarrassed, and are happy that they did not succeed. The drawings of the concrete monstrosity that was to replace Bryggen have simply gathered dust.

Bryggen was once 300 metres long. The 58 remaining buildings represent an architectural tradition which dates back almost nine hundred years. Such wooden clusters were once a common sight in many European harbour towns.

Bryggen is a living treasure which is on UNESCO's World Heritage List. Artists and craftsmen, translators and fashion designers, architects and stone sellers now occupy the workshops and stores where Hanseatic tradesmen once kept dried fish and other goods. There are also cosy pubs and first-class restaurants with dangerously tilting original floors.

The narrow wood-paved passages between the long buildings invite you away from the harbour, as if to pull you deep into Bryggen's past. Bryggen was the economic centre of Bergen from the time the city was founded in around 1070. From 1360, Hanseatic tradesmen dominated the activity of Bryggen; at times there were as many as 2000 Germans residing in Bergen, mostly involved in the export of dried fish. For centuries, services in German were held in the nearby St. Mary's Church, the oldest in Bergen, built in the mid 12th century.

Seven major fires have caused much destruction. After each fire, Bryggen was re-built in accordance with the original pattern. The present buildings date back to 1702. In 1955, a devastating fire destroyed nearly half of the buildings. Archaeologists used the opportunity to dig down into the layers underneath the ashes. Bryggen is built on debris which has accumulated over many centuries. The harbour waters once reached almost 150 metres further inland than today. At Bryggen Museum at the north end of Bryggen, these finds are preserved – ceramics and glass from many countries on the continent attest to trade links as early as the 12th century.

From behind Bryggen, we look down on its fifth facade, a patchwork of slate roofs, ceramic tiles and corrugated steel. Surprising to all but appreciative locals, there is also a reconstructed herb garden, benches and beautiful rose beds tucked away in the back.

Top: An old ledger used by a tradesman. From the Hanseatic Museum.

The wood-paved alleyways of Bryggen beckon you deeply into its living history.

The sculptures above the alleyways that lead inside Bryggen were not just for decoration; they made it easy for those who could not read to find the right address.

The faces of many old people along the coast show a well-lived life, and eyes that glow with gratitude and the wisdom learned from changing seasons.

Flåmsbana

Railway connoisseurs consider Flåmsbana the most exciting railway ride in all of Europe. On its 20 km journey, the Flåmsbana railway passes through 20 tunnels with gradients up to 1:18. The difference in altitude between Myrdal and Flåm is all of 865 metres. The railway took 20 years to build and was actually completed in 1940 by the Germans who occupied Norway.

The first stretch after you leave Myrdal station may seem ordinary. The drama begins as soon as the train starts its descent down the Flåm valley. The railway line traverses deep canyons, hugs mountain shelves, speeds in and out of tunnels, passes snow-topped mountains and offers lush views of the green valley below. It's a glorious, constantly changing 40-minute panorama.

Kjosfossen falls, at which the train always stops in the summer, must be the most photographed waterfall in all of Norway. But the best view of the railway itself is gained by bicycling or walking the old construction road, at your own chosen pace.

The Flåmsbana railway, a side track of the Bergen railway, is rightly considered one of the finest rides in Europe!

Three Northern Towns

Ålesund is famous not only for its harmonious Art Nouveau architecture, but also for its beautiful seaside setting.

The three northernmost towns of Fjord Norway have a charm all their own. After the town burned down in the tragic fire of 1904, Ålesund was rebuilt in Jugendstil (art nouveau) architecture. It is now a candidate for UNESCO's World Heritage list. After the catastrophe, which left 800 buildings in ashes and ten thousand people homeless, Emperor Wilhelm II of Germany offered his help. Four ships filled with food and medicine, blankets and building supplies, originally destined for one of the German colonies, was ordered to sail full speed to Ålesund.

There is a standing joke about the thrifty, industrious people of Sunnmøre: If one of them is washed up on a deserted island after a shipwreck, and you sail to fetch him a month later, he will have built a furniture factory and a chapel!

Traditions are intact; the region accounts for more than three quarters of the furniture made in Norway. Ekornes still produces its famous Stressless chairs, introduced in 1971 and providing comfort for the weary backs of more than five million purchasers world-wide, at its factory 40 km southeast of Ålesund. They are not alone in offering quality products; the region of Sunnmøre accounts for more than three quarters of the furniture produced in Norway.

Molde is known for jazz, roses and its gorgeous panorama. Those with the patience to count claim you can see 87 mountain peaks, which of course says a lot about the wilderness adventures waiting nearby.

The history of modern jazz can be written simply on the basis of the great musicians who have played at Molde's famous jazz festival; there are few omissions. Molde is also known as the "town of roses". Those tempted to point out that there are more impressive rose gardens in France, for instance, would do well to remember that Molde lies at an altitude further north than Anchorage, Alaska!

Travellers who are not fortunate enough to be cruising Norwegian waters definitely have to choose the coastal route when driving from Molde to Kristiansund – and the route is most exciting on a windy day! Eight bridges take you across islands and skerries. With the fjord at your right and the sea at your left, you sometimes feel as though you are driving on water, especially if a stiff gale and huge breakers drench your car. This is not always the place for a convertible!

The Gulf Stream keeps all Norwegian coastal ports free of ice and contributes to the rich fisheries that were the first source of the region's prosperity. While there are sizeable fishing fleets supplying fish exporters in Ålesund and Molde as well, it is Kristiansund which is known for klipfish. In the olden days, the families of fishermen lay cod and other fish on cliffs to dry in the sun, whereas in Lofoten – also known for its dried cod – they built long racks to accommodate their catch. Be sure to taste the result at one of Kristiansund's fine restaurants, where bacalao is just one of the dishes made with klipfish.

Molde is sometimes called "the town of roses".

Skiing with Molde's famous panorama of 87 mountains in the distance.

Kristiansund is built on islands linked by bridges. "Lofotkompaniet" has been dealing in dried cod for generations.

Glaciers – The Ice that Sculpted the Fjords

The Jostedal glacier covers approximately 490 km². It is the largest mainland glacier in Europe. But its beauty, which has fascinated countless travellers, is not a question of statistics.

The famous English mountaineer, William Cecil Slingsby, described Jostedal glacier as "the finest ice scenery in Europe". At the end of the 19th century, however, he wasn't the first to traverse this vast expanse of ice. Centuries before him, villagers crossed the glacier to take part in church services or weddings, drive cattle across to willing buyers, or to court available members of the opposite sex.

Exhibitions at the Norwegian Glacier Museum in Fjærland, and at the Glacier Centre in Jostedalen, tell the story of the glacier and of the people who first dared to explore it. On the Jostedal glacier, even on the hottest summer day, you can go skiing in shorts or bikini! The adventurous may spend a few hours on the glacier on foot with an experienced guide. But never approach the ice without a guide – unless you want to risk a once-in-a-lifetime experience!

A sheet of ice up to 3 km thick once covered most of northern Europe. This ice carved out the valleys and fjords of western Norway, scouring the land clean, patiently gnawing at mountainsides. As it grew warmer, the retreating ice deposited minerals that nourished the first plants. Slowly the soil was rebuilt. Today, the valleys near the Jostedal glacier are surprisingly fertile, with a rich and varied vegetation.

The ice of the glacier is not eternal; the oldest ice in the Jostedal glacier is "only" 5000 years old. The most recent Ice Age began 70-80 000 years ago, but 6-7000 years ago, the area was freed of ice. In fact, there have been at least 40 ice ages during the last 2.5 million years. The Jostedal glacier has grown and shrunk with the changes in climate. When large volumes of snow add massive weight, faster than it can melt, the glacier's arms are rolled out like baker's dough. In the last seven years, Briksdalsbreen has been lengthened by more than 500 metres.

Each year an average of 5-6 m of snow falls on the glacier. Snow crystals are like microscopic ornaments of six-fold symmetry. Gradually these crystals are pressed into corn snow and then firn, which is more compact and contains little air. In the course of years, firn is compressed into dense, glacial ice.

Near the glacier, the noise of civilisation is distant, but the glacier itself is full of sound. There is a loud explosion when a section cracks off an icefall. Chunks of ice are pounded and pulverised where a glacier moves down a slope, and by a glacier river raging with meltwater, you may hear a deep rumble as large stones are rolled and shoved along the bottom.

The Trees and Forests

Ferns are some of the world's oldest plants. 300 million years ago, they covered much of our planet.

Five to eight thousand years ago, when the climate of Norway was much milder than it is today, there were large forests of warmth-loving trees. In sheltered valleys and on the sunny northern shores of fjords, there are still groves or even small forests of oak trees, beech, linden or hazel. The clusters of such trees near the ruins of monasteries, however, were probably planted by monks.

During the 17th and 18th centuries, there was a large-scale export of timber from western Norway. Much of London and Amsterdam was built of Norwegian wood, before bricks and concrete got their heyday.

Near Nordfjord, there are forests of juniper that are large as pines. The northern-most naturally growing beech forest stands at Seim, in the municipality of Lindås north of Bergen. Here and there along the coast, there are also forests of fir, often with straight boundaries. They are not native here and do not really fit into the landscape.

Up near the tree line, dwarf birch also form a forest of sorts, even though it may be only man height.

Often it is solitary trees that impress us – the twisted pine that weathers the storm on its promontory, or the one that seems to defy gravity on a sheer cliff, finding nourishment and support by sinking roots into the smallest of cracks, even prying them wider.

A lush forest along the Rauma river.

The Mountains

Peering into the abyss from Pulpit Rock.

The awesome roar and power of waterfalls have fascinated and cleansed ramblers since time immemorial.

Far right: The snow-covered Sunnmøre Alps.

Mountains? It's far easier to list the places in Fjord Norway devoid of mountains! The differing height, form and vegetation of mountains speak of their geological history – and that history is complex. Some mountains consist of rock more than a billion years old, but surprisingly, many were cut and ground into their present form only during the last 2.5 million years. The sculptor, of course, was the inland ice that covered most of Scandinavia.

The Lysefjord and Geirangerfjord both have seaside cliffs called Preikestolen, Pulpit Rock, the former more impressive and famous, rising a sheer 600 m from the fjord. Generally, hills and mountains become rounder as you move eastward.

The mountains explain why it costs a fortune to build roads in the west of Norway; you have to either go around them or blast tunnels through them – our forefathers solved the problem by rowing or sailing to many of their destinations. Those on a car holiday risk getting the "inside view" of Fjord Norway if they insist on taking the straightest roads – far better to choose the older ones that meander like rivers.

During the Easter holidays, there is a mass exodus of Norwegians from towns and cities. They head for the mountains laden with ski equipment, sunglasses and warm sweaters.

Most Norwegians are well aware of their privileged surroundings and make good use of the wilderness. To accommodate them, there is a fine system of mountain lodges.

More than a few unconsciously view the mountains as fixed points in their existence, and hence return to them regularly for renewal. It's been said that when the church tries to count its congregation, it should include most of those who seek the silence of the mountains – after all, prayer is an act of the listening heart.

Birds and Bird Cliffs

Fishermen bring tourists up close to the bird clirfs.

Top: The ever-watchful sea eagle.

Left: A puffin takes a brief rest before returning to the nest to feed its offspring. There is competition for food when thousands of them nest on the same bird cliff!

Patience and a good zoom lens are called for if you want to capture the birds onto film.

As a result of the Gulf Stream and the mild winters in Norway's coastal regions, many bird species are observed farther north than elsewhere in the world. The whooper swan, once almost extinct in Europe, has recently begun expanding southward from its traditional nesting sites in northernmost Scandinavia.

Fishermen are often guided by the behaviour of birds when they cast their nets. Seagulls and other seabirds stick around after fishing boats arrive, waiting for tasty morsels to be tossed their way as the catch is cleaned. Excavation of a number of dwelling caves has revealed that our ancestors often hunted sea birds. Until a century or so ago, it was not uncommon for people to gather the eggs or kill the offspring of auks, cormorants and even seagulls for food. Grouse, capercaillie and ptarmigan are still considered fine game for the dinner table.

One of the most fascinating coastal birds is the puffin, sometimes called the "sea parrot" because of its colourful beak. The willow grouse on the islands of Smøla have adapted to the mild winters. Here, they no longer don white feathers, as they do to blend in with the snowy inland areas.

Norway's national bird is the dipper, a relatively small and humble bird which snaps up insects and small animals in the river rapids and waterfalls. As a result, it thrives throughout almost all of Norway.

240 bird species have been observed at Runde, more than at any other bird cliff along the Norwegian coast. Runde, which lies west of Ålesund, is sometimes referred to as the avian metropolis by the sea. Of course the birds are just as likely to be scrutinising their human audience as well.

Hundreds of conservation areas have been set aside for birds up and down the coast, not all of them large and impressive at first glance. There may be some very distinct bird locales within a rather small area. While one area may be exposed, there may be a protected pocket around a promontory, tucked away in a fjord arm or sheltered by an island. Woodlands may be filled with one kind of song, while marshlands offer very different bird calls.

Norway – Below the Surface of the Sea

Top: The colourful plumose anemone

Even the heart of an experience diver beats faster when he or she explores underwater caves!

So you have seen most of what Fjord Norway has to offer? Bergen and the Geirangerfjord, Pulpit Rock, the mountains of Romsdal, the myriad of islands up and down the coast… But have you ever explored the underwater caves at Stad, investigated old ship wrecks, admired colourful sea anemones and watched plants sway in tidal currents? And have you brought up scallops and wolffish for a feast with friends?

Amongst connoisseurs, Norway has long had a reputation as one of the world's most exciting diving paradises. In its own way, our coastal waters are just as exotic as more tropical seas. Did you know that the last World Championships in Underwater Photography of the last millennium were held outside Ålesund?

"I have dived in many seas, and many famous sites have impressed me with their beauty. Nevertheless, if I had to make a choice, I would choose the coastal waters of Norway – including Spitzbergen, mind you." Per Eide knows what he's talking about. He took the photographs on these pages and those in the rest of this book; he is also four-time Nordic champion in underwater photography.

Underwater fjord views can be just as impressive as the famous landscape above the waterline familiar to tourists. Sheer cliffs plunge into black depths – Sognefjord is more than 1300 metres deep. There are caves and crevasses, screes and overhangs.

Every season shows the diver something new. Sunny summer days bring out the glow in the colours of undersea flora and fauna. Early autumn, when there are less algae, is an even better time to explore this silent world. In winter, colours fade and even underwater plants seem to wither. Everything looks desolate.

"That's when I have the sea to myself. Visibility may be as much as 50 metres, and I feel as though I am a privileged witness to a secret world when winter light creates magical patterns in the water column," says Per Eide.

In March and April, algae blossom again, providing nourishment for fish and animals that suddenly emerge from their hiding places. Colours return to the undersea world of Norway as well.

There probably still are silver and gold coins near the wreck of the Akerendam, which sank near Runde in 1725. Here, in 1974, at a depth of less than ten metres, divers brought up more than 700 kilos of precious metals. Even if you don't discover gold, you may be lucky enough to see a puffin or cormorant dive for its dinner.

Hustadvika, between Molde and Kristiansund, is special for other reasons. Impressive underwater rock formations, a kelp forest, and the unusually varied fauna, which includes a seal colony, have put this area on the short list for future national parks. Even without diving equipment, you can get a good impression of what it's like by visiting the aquarium outside Ålesund or the one in Bergen.

"One of my favourite dives is in the magnificent Norangsdalen. In 1908, an avalanche dammed up the river. Within a week, the mountain farm and the old road between Øye and Hellesylt were submerged. It feels quite unusual to swim along the trunk road and stone bridges, and to see the fragile remnants of trees that grew here, " says Per Eide.

The Cultural Landscape

The Norwegian pony has helped farmers pull many heavy burdens through the centuries. Fræna.

To cows, green is a flavour, not a colour! At Horr, Jæren.

The landscape formed by mankind's efforts to make ends meet, through generations and centuries, is called the cultural landscape.

Twelve thousand years ago, much of Norway was covered with ice. Only a few narrow stretches along the coast saw sunlight, and some mountain peaks were tall enough to protrude through the icy wasteland. The soil of the Norwegian coast is still young and in many places very sparse and thin. Even cultivated land is often broken by rocks, boulders and crags. Here and there groves of trees also seem like islands of the original landscape.

From the air, it may seem that Norwegians have left their marks on but a fraction of the land. On closer inspection, there are many traces, though it may require a slow tempo and knowledgeable eyes to see them.

The trained eye sees old hunting pits, vegetation changed by centuries of grazing near mountain farms, old burial mounds and outlines of the foundations of ancient dwellings. It makes out stone walls overgrown with moss supporting terraces of tilled land, slabs of slate leading across brooks to old elm trees with short trunks and many low branches that were once harvested for feed, and cotters' farms reclaimed by the forest.

The vast and open heather-clad heathlands are not wilderness, rather they a landscape formed by man, which once stretched all the way from northern Spain to the

A road leads to the mountain farms in Nordstølheia.

Old traditions are still maintained at the Herdalsseter mountain farm in Norddal.

Lofoten islands. There were once lush forests many places along the coast and on many islands that are now barren. Through the centuries before history was written, people burned many of them and planted in the ashes. Gradually, farming became more important than hunting and gathering, but most farmer families still augmented their diet by fishing. The newly established Heathland Centre at Lygra, north of Bergen, yields insight into this rich history.

Archaelogists have speculated as to why they haven't found more farms and settlements from the Viking period. The simple explanation may be that many contemporary farm buildings are built right on top of the old ruins.

A few old hamlets remain, such as Agatunet and Havråtunet. In 1837, a new law radically changed inheritance rules, farm land was kept more intact and farmers moved their houses out of village clusters onto their own land.

No one knows how many miles of rock walls divide up this land. For those who want to immerse themselves, there are endless volumes of local history detailing what is known about each farm. Of course knowledge and collective memory only stretch so far back into the mists of time. Much is waiting to be discovered even to the trained eye.

The Vikings

Top: Jewellery, a sword, spear and axes once used for defence – or perhaps in one of the many Viking attacks on foreign shores.

King Harald V and Queen Sonja onboard "Borgundknarren", a reconstruction of a Viking ship.

Horns are blown to warn of the arrival of enemy ships!

The reputation of Vikings as plundering barbarians, who just happened to be master boatbuilders, is considerably exaggerated. By and large the Viking period saw a peaceful development, and most of the goods and treasures that the Vikings brought home were acquired through honest barter.

On the other hand, there is no denying that they did carry out gruesome attacks which gave people good reason to fear them, and their violent reputations may sometimes have given them the better bargain. The attack on an unprotected monastery on the island of Lindisfarne near the Scottish border in 793 is generally considered the start of the Viking period. But history may have to be rewritten; two of the twelve ship graves that have thus far been discovered in Europe were found in Avaldsnes – and one of them, containing a 25 metre long ship, was from 690-750, indicating that the Viking period began far earlier than previously believed.

A considerable population increase may have caused the exodus and exploration of the Vikings. But we also know that social structures were becoming more complex, giving rise to the dawn of nationhood. The sagas tell of a number of chieftains who had to flee after losing a power struggle.

Leif Eiriksson's discovery of Vinland – America – some 500 years before Christopher Columbus is well-documented. The Vikings also settled the Orkney and Shetland islands, the Hebrides and the Isle of Man, Iceland and Greenland, the coast of Normandy and much of the British Isles and Ireland. In fact, Dublin was founded by the Viking chieftain Olav the White in 850. Viking ornamentation is only one indication that the Norsemen had extensive contact with the Celts and were strongly influenced by them.

The Norsemen navigated the Rhine, sailed up the Volga through Russia, all the way to the distant shore of the Caspian Sea, before crossing to Baghdad on foot. Or

There are hundreds of grave mounds along the coast, some pre-dating the Vikings. This one is at Løsethstranda on the island of Gurskøy.

Did you know that most days of the week are named after old Norse gods?

they rounded the Straits of Gibraltar, visited the Mediterranean countries and reached the Middle East by sea. They acquired Arabic glass, rich treasures of coins and silver, Persian ceramics and Irish bronze. They traded away furs and honey, vessels of soapstone and even slaves.

Viking silversmiths made jewellery of lasting beauty. Colourful glass beads, often with sophisticated patterns, were also in great demand, as was amber. Viking women of high status were buried with incomparable treasures.

There were Viking tradeswomen as well as tradesmen; women had strong and in many respects equally important social roles. That only changed with the introduction of Christianity and continental ideas about new ideals for women.

The Viking Ship Museum in Oslo contains far more than ships. The richly ornamented ceremonial carriage, as well as sleds once drawn by horses, found at Oseberg, provide a visual feast.

The restored Viking farm at Avaldsnes on Karmøy in southwestern Norway, is immensely popular with school children as well as tourists. Here, the history of the Norsemen is brought to life. All the inventory is based on archaeological finds and careful research.

At Borg in Lofoten, there is a Viking museum with a reconstructed longhouse that is more than 80 metres long! Here many visitors have enjoyed a real Viking feast, although parties a thousand years ago were said to be much wilder indeed!

The Stave Churches

Hopperstad stave church was puchased and lovingly restored by the architect P. Blix – at his own expense. He couldn't bear the thought of the local congregation wanting to tear it down.

Top: 140 portals have been wholly or partly preserved. These beautiful carvings of intertwined animals are from Urnes, the oldest stave church still standing.

Interior of Kvernes stave church, with traditional floral decorations from 1630–40 covering almost every inch of the walls and ceiling. The ship model is just as old. A ship decorates many Norwegian churches.

One of the world's foremost cultural monument lies on a small headland overlooking an arm of the Sognefjord. Urnes, which is the oldest of Norway's stave churches and has changed little since 1150, is on UNESCO's World Heritage List.

The excellent condition of these wooden churches is a fine testimony to the skilled craftsmen that built them 7-800 years ago. In fact, the time-honoured techniques of Viking boat builders were used to prepare materials for the stave churches. Years before the felling of slow-growing pines, the bark would be removed from the lower part of the trunk, or the top would be cut off. As a result, the wood would be filled with resin, making it very resistant to rot. In addition, the stave churches were regularly treated with tar.

On the most complex stave churches – such as Urnes, Borgund and Hopperstad – we see gable upon gable rise to a crowning spire, giving them their very characteristic shape. Not all of them are so impressive; Undredal stave church near Aurland is less than 4 metres wide.

The stave churches' elevated nave, arcades and columns ending in cubed capitals are reminiscent of Romanesque stone churches. Some experts, however, are convinced that their architecture is based on the Pre-Christian style and construction methods of the Vikings. Nor is it far-fetched to see a Celtic influence. The carvings on the portals – especially the intertwined, stylised animals at Urnes – bear a remarkable resemblance to the ornamentation found in the Irish Book of Kells. Irish monks and missionaries travelled to Norway centuries before 1030, the date officially used for the introduction of Christianity, and we also know that the Vikings brought back Irish servants and craftsmen.

There is much evidence that the stave churches were prefabricated and the standardised parts quickly erected by specialised craftsmen. It is estimated that 2000 such churches were built during 1150-1350, an average of ten each year. Even though stone was considered a more noble material, Norwegians insisted on building the vast majority of their churches of wood.

The use of staves, or vertically placed lumber, to build self-supporting walls was once a common construction method throughout much of northern Europe.

The Black Death of 1350, which killed more than half of Norway's population, was also a hard blow to the maintenance of the stave churches. By 1650 there were 270 left, and in 1850 only 60 were still standing. Many of these were bought by individuals or museums who wished to preserve and restore them. Today, there are 28 stave churches left in Norway. In addition, the stave church at Fantoft outside Bergen, which burned down in 1992, has been painstakingly rebuilt using traditional techniques.

As a point of curiosity, the stave church from Vang in Valdres now stands in Riesengebirge, Poland. It was given to the poor congregation of this mountain village by a Prussian prince. Eager American descendants of Norwegian emigrants have built several copies of stave churches, including a full-scale copy of Borgund in Rapid City, South Dakota.

The Boat Building Tradition

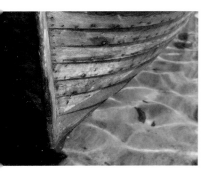

Petroglyphs from the island of Østre Åmøy, north of Stavanger.

The secrets of boat building have been handed down through generations for more than a thousand years. Sigurd Bjørkedal and his three sons in the process of building a copy of the Gokstad ship.

Ever since the Vikings set sail in their longboats, Norway has been justly famous for the excellent craftsmanship of its boatbuilders. Archaeological finds indicate that the tradition is far older than the Vikings, although they refined boat building to an art. Anyone who visits the Viking Ship Museum outside Oslo is struck by the elegance of their old ships. The smaller rowboats that were found with the Gokstad ship bear a remarkable resemblance to the Oselvar, still being built in the district south of Bergen.

Hull designs and rudder fittings suggest that sails were not in use until the 8th century, almost 4000 years after the Egyptians and Mesopotamians made use of the wind. But the Norwegians caught on quickly and were soon sailing remarkably sturdy vessels far and wide.

We know from the sagas that ships as long as 40 metres were built for Olav Tryggvason. The master boat builders in Bjørkedal have built several copies of Viking ships for the adventurer Ragnar Thorseth, who has been intent on proving their seaworthiness. Sturdy boats were the Vikings' only form of insurance against rough seas.

A broad-headed axe is one of the most important tools for the traditional boat builder. So is the angled plumb, which is used to check that the boards are at the correct angles in all places. The boards are carefully braced in place with sticks wedged against the ceiling and floor of the shop, giving the boat its proper form. Then holes are drilled and copper or iron rivets put into place, and a precisely shaped ribbed frame is added for strength.

Surprisingly, many boats are built relatively far inland, near mature forests of slow-grown pines. In some districts, hardwoods such as oak or birch were used for

exposed or vulnerable parts. The famous Oseberg ship was built entirely of oak. Specially shaped materials were used as ribs and rowlocks, for instance. The boat builders knew their forests well and could afford to wait for a tree with a desirable curved root or branch to reach its ideal size.

Preparation of materials would start even before a tree was felled. Perhaps bark was stripped off up to the branches, or the top of the tree was cut off, so that the trunk would fill with resin. Sometimes the materials were submerged in the sea or in marshes for a year or two. Any materials showing signs of rot were discarded. The most vulnerable places on a ship, such as the end grain of ribbing, were drilled and filled with sea salt to prevent rotting.

Many old ships and boats have been restored to seaworthiness at Mellomværftet, the boatyard at Nordmøre Museum, in the town of Kristiansund. Also at Norheim-sund in Hardanger, there is a centre for the protection of old vessels. In addition many proud boat owners have restored old fishing smacks, Hardanger sloops and other boats and vessels no longer being produced at modern boatyards.

It's quite a sight when harbours are filled with old wooden boats. The Market Days (Torgdagene) in Bergen and the Harbour Days in Haugesund are just two such cultural events that are not to be missed!

Time-Honoured Building Methods

"Norway... isn't that where they build houses of wood!?" The question was posed by a man from Greece, which had plenty of its own forests three thousand years ago. In most regions of Norway, wood is plentiful. Except for in the inner cities, most houses in Norway are built of wood; in many other countries, this is a prohibitively expensive material which only the rich can afford.

Log houses and cog joints required patience and mastery of the axe. Century-old farm buildings of untreated wood show little tarnish of time. Hidden underneath the panelling of refurbished houses, there are often joints that a modern carpenter would be hard-pressed to reproduce

Longhouses, in which people people and animals each inhabited an end, were once quite common. It was convenient, as the chores were never far away, and the animals provided some warmth in the winter. Here and there you may notice the exposed wall of barns or old houses is protected by carefully piled stone.

Turf roofs are still popular, although today birch bark is just used for trimmings at the edge. Some of the old ones may have beautiful collections of flowers and even a tree or two growing out of them. In some districts, the walls of barns were sometimes constructed by tying bundles of juniper branches together. The lower parts of the wall might simply be slabs of slate stood on end.

Building methods vary from place to place in Fjord Norway, according to traditions that have arisen from materials available. On many farms, archaeologists could probably dig down through layers and find signs of continuous habitations stretching back a thousand years or more.

Juniper branches are woven in order to insulate a barn wall at Havråtunet.

Modern houses, too, are often built of nature's finest building materials.

The church and a traditional house in Eikesdal, Nordmøre.

Small photo, next page:
Cogging joints of untreated logs have stood the test of time beneath this roof of rough-hewn slate. Fitjadalen.

Prior to the new Land Laws of
1937, there were many villages
and hamlets like Agatunet.
(Top and right)

Traditional Costume – the Bunad

The traditional costume of Norway, the "bunad", is complex and costly clothing – unless of course you are lucky enough to inherit one or have chosen to spend the many hours required to make it properly. Traditions are being renewed; many girls receive a bunad just prior to their confirmation. It's a costume she will treasure and wear for special occasions for many years. The floral borders of skirts, bright linen shirts, colourful bead-embellished bodices and beautifully embroidered shawls make this seem like royal garb.

There are bunads for men too, but they're not worn nearly so often. Some men do, however, don this finery when they take a bride.

Norwegian peasants and farmers were considerably better off than their counterparts elsewhere in Europe. Tradition dictated that a farmer's daughter be a princess when she weds. She even wore a richly ornamented silver crown! "The Wedding Procession in Hardanger", painted by Adolph Tidemand and Hans Fredrik Gude in 1848 and which now hangs in the National Gallery, shows this time-honoured dress in all its detail. It has virtually become Norway's national painting.

On closer inspection, you may be astounded at the treasure of silver displayed. The accessories are an integral part of the bunad, as is the knife too. Notice also the complicated weaving techniques, decorations of minute glass beads, and time-consuming embroideries and specialised stitchwork. It takes hundreds of hours to make a bunad in the old-fashioned way!

In the decades prior to 1839, rural silversmiths were actually outlawed. The craft guilds in the towns and cities had a total monopoly of the market – at least in theory.

There is a rich symbolism in the jewellery. The stylised letters "AM" stand for Ave Maria, while the often repeated ring or circle symbolises eternity and creation. Many of the larger brooches have a beautiful six-fold symmetry, like exquisite snowflakes.

Toward the end of the 19th century, the National Romantics inspired a new appreciation of the Norwegian peasant culture. Two women played a decisive role in revitalising the folk costume traditions: Hulda Garborg and Klara Semb. Since a proper bunad is based on the finery and everyday clothing worn by people in specific areas, each region in Norway now has its own bunad, sometimes with intriguing variations. The costumes worn by peasants were inspired by Renaissance clothing common on the continent in the 16th and 17th centuries; in some regions there is a continuous tradition extending right up to modern times, while the bunads of other areas may be reconstructions based on rather sketchy historical material.

A comparison of bunads worn today with those in museums reveals the influence of modern fashions and materials. The blouses are thinner, the cut slightly adjusted, and the waist lowered.

No one is able to say exactly how many different bunads there are in Norway. Since this living folk tradition is not based on precise formulas, there are many variations on each of them.

The traditional costume of Hardanger, with its colourful beadwork, is the best-known of Norway's bunads.

The apron of the Hardanger bunad.

There are many variations on the
Sunnmøre bunad, from the region
of Ørsta and Volda; these are just
a few.

The Sound of Norway – The Hardanger Fiddle

A skilful fiddle maker takes pride in his signature decorations, and sometimes has the help of the finest artist in the district.

Sympathetic strings give the Hardanger fiddle a magical sound all its own. It may look like a violin, but recent research indicates this fiddle has other ancestors.

For many people, the opening ceremony of the 1994 Winter Olympics in Lillehammer was the first time they heard the magical sound of the Hardanger fiddle. As dancers in colourful national costumes swirled on the snow, fiddlers in horse-drawn sleds played until their sweat poured forth.

As in other countries, Norwegian folk music has always been closely associated with festivities, dance and ritual. The very term itself lets it be known that this music belongs to the people; folk music is an integral part of life. The Hardanger fiddle's close association with dance and festivities almost did the instrument in. Festivities? Rather drunkenness, irresponsibility and immorality – or so claimed preachers of the puritanical movements that swept Western Norway in the 19th century.

The Hardanger fiddle is usually decorated with black-ink floral paintings on the body, and inlaid mother-of-pearl on its edge and fingerboard. The beautifully carved head of a dragon, woman or lion that rounds off the neck is often the signature and pride of the fiddle maker.

Of course, it is the sound that sets the Hardanger fiddle apart from the violin. As the fiddler draws his bow across perhaps two or three strings, the 4-5 sympathetic strings just under them resonate, lending the music an ethereal quality. Melody and drone are interwoven in a magical tapestry of sound. And the complex rhythms may change several times in the middle of a tune.

In 1849, the classical violinist Ole Bull, who was famous throughout all of Europe, brought the legendary fiddler Torgeir Augundsen to play a concert with him in the capital. But the ears of the capital's cosmopolitan concert-goers were definitely not tuned to the unusual sound of changing rhythms and tones drifting in the intervals that formed the accepted scale of classical and church music. Folk music was not for the elite.

Perhaps the Hardanger fiddle needs the mountains around it to echo properly. It needs the wind rustling in old birch and pine; it needs the crystal clear river singing its way to the ocean. On the other hand, if you close your eyes when a master fiddler strokes the bow across the strings, all this and more will take form before your inner eye!

Perhaps that is what inspired Edvard Grieg to transcribe many folk melodies and arrange piano music based on them; most notable is Opus 72, which really should be heard juxtaposed with the fiddle music that inspired it. Grieg tuned his music to the spirit that lived in the folk music traditions. Today, to listeners of classical music all over the world, Norway is inseparable from Grieg's music.

Although there has never been a greater interest in Norwegian folk music than there is now, folk music is forced to find new venues – the old contexts are gone. The challenge for folk musicians is to stay in tune with the spirit of tradition without allowing the music to stiffen into folklore.

Even today, much of the renewal of Norwegian traditional music happens at the cutting edge, when it meets other music forms, such as jazz and the folk music of other countries. Researchers, music lovers, and the musicians themselves are often astonished at how close parallels there are between native music from different parts of the world.

Reach for the Sky!

There are excellent climbing areas throughout western Norway. The best known, but also the most difficult, is the 1100 metre high rock wall of Trollveggen. In 1967, it took a French team 20 days to conquer a direct route to the top!

Not far away are the magnificent Sunnmøre Alps and the challenging Romsdal mountain range. Further south, along the Lysefjord east of Stavanger, there are plenty of challenges near Kjerag and Preikestolen, better known as Pulpit Rock.

The Norwegian climbing milieu abides by clear aesthetic and ethical principles. Leave no traces – no pegs, pitons, rope. Change yourself, not the mountain, for the mountains will be here long after the letters have faded from our gravestones.

Of course, you don't have to insist on the most death-defying route in order to reach for the sky. Take Trollveggen, for instance; a relaxing 3-4 hour trek from the back side takes you to the top, and the view is just as great as if you had gotten there hauling yourself up inch by inch by fingertips and rope. Sometimes you can see a paraglider aloft high above the valley floor. But it's quite dangerous – and illegal – to leap from the mountaintop.

It's worth taking a closer look at the rock under your feet. In the Tafjord mountains near the Geirangerfjord, there is a rare and colourful rock called eclogite, which consists of reddish-violet garnet crystals, yellowish-green olivine and grass-green pyroxene. In many places in western Norway, you can see rockfaces polished smooth or showing scouring marks left by gravel imbedded in the vast sheet of ice that

ground them down during successive Ice Ages, the most recent only ten thousand years ago.

All throughout Norway, and especially in the mountainous areas, there are well-equipped lodges. Some of them even serve tasty dinners!

For the sofa mountaineer, it's well worth going back to read the writings of William Cecil Slingsby, a mountain pioneer who explored many of Norway's finest climbing areas.

If you don't enjoy the heights, you can always don a wetsuit and dive into the depths; there are fine coastal waters to explore along most of western Norway. Or try kayaking into a tranquil sunset. For a wilder water sport, you can always try rafting on the river rapids. Summer never stopped the true ski buff – at least not in Fjord Norway where there are several summer ski resorts.

Fishing the Rivers and Sea

There are many ancient petroglyphs of fish along the Norwegian coast. Since long before man settled the first areas freed of ice more than ten thousand years ago, the Gulf Stream has swept warm waters toward the nutrient-rich waters off Norway. Even the historians of ancient Greece found reason to comment on the unusually rich fishing in these waters.

If you throw a hook into the Norwegian sea or fjords, you have to be quite unlucky not to haul up a catch. There is plenty of cod, saithe, haddock, mackerel and dozens of other species to satisfy everybody. To be in an open boat the midst of a school of mackerel, for example, is an unforgettable experience. These fast swimmers put up an energetic fight and it's not unusual to catch one on every hook.

The importance of fish can hardly be exaggerated. It is said that both Haugesund and Stavanger are built on herring bones; much of western Norway experienced a new-found prosperity thanks to the unusually rich herring fisheries during the latter half of the 19th century. Bergen would not have become what it is today without the Hanseatic traders, who for centuries made fortunes exporting dried cod from Lofoten to the continent. And few would have bothered to settle the islands of Lofoten in centuries past if there had been no fish to catch offshore. As in centuries past, there is still a Klondike atmosphere in the winter, when vast numbers of mature cod arrive from the Barents Sea to spawn.

No one knows how far the traditions of drying fish date back in Lofoten or on the Møre coast. In other places, fish was sometimes dug down into the snow or frozen in ice where it would keep well during the winter.

In the middle of the 19th century, wealthy English adventurers discovered the huge salmon that migrated up the rivers of western Norway to spawn. They were astonished to hook specimens weighing more than 30 kilos. These visitors didn't wait long to negotiate fishing rights with the farmers, returning year after year to enjoy the stunning beauty of crystal clear rivers, verdant valleys and wild mountains. The lords and career military officers must have been quite a sight when they arrived by horse and fancy wagons, or in large private yachts. A few Scottish and English families still lease the solitary right to fish certain stretches of the best salmon rivers during the summer.

Each river has its own salmon stock and the differences between them can be quite visible. It is still a mystery how the salmon manage to find their way up rivers and back to precisely the tributary in which they were hatched. One theory is that they follow a faint scent trail left by smolt which swim out to sea just before they themselves swim upstream at the end of May and beginning of June.

The best-known salmon rivers are Suldalslågen, Vosso, Rauma and Stryn, Tana and Alta – and the Lærdal river, to which King Harald V of Norway has returned almost every year, since catching his first salmon at age 15.

Norwegians are a practical people and have developed many contraptions to catch salmon. One of them is the "laksegilje", a small elevated hut from which a fisherman could keep an eye on a netbag placed in a narrow fjord arm. When he saw the salmon swim into it, all he had to do was pull a rope to close it off. In other places, fishermen placed traps in the river, into which salmon and trout could swim in but not out.

Top: Salmon (Salmo salar) is the king of freshwater fish.

A fly-fisherman tests her luck in Lake Lovatnet.

The cod near Stad can reach trophy size.

Five fishermen are ready to prepare their catch above the fire by Nosvatnet in Nordmøre. Eide.

Trout fishing is a far less costly sport than salmon fishing. In Norway, there are many rivers and tributaries, and thousands of lakes where you can enjoy solitude and magnificent scenery while testing your luck. More than a few chefs admit that the best way to enjoy trout is to cook it over an open fire, perhaps adding a few wild herbs. Even if none should strike at your line, you're more than likely to return with a satisfied smile at day's end.

Festivals and Museums

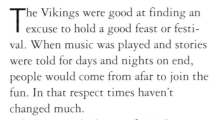

The Vikings were good at finding an excuse to hold a good feast or festival. When music was played and stories were told for days and nights on end, people would come from afar to join the fun. In that respect times haven't changed much.

Summer is the hottest festival season. For those who appreciate folk music, a highlight is the Førde Folk Music Festival. Stavanger is well-known for its International Chamber Music Festival, where concerts are even held in a 13th century monastery. The Bergen Festival dates back to a music festival that Edvard Grieg helped organise in 1898. Parallel events include concerts of contemporary music and a jazz festival. When it comes to jazz, however, the town where it really swings is Molde, in the middle of July.

There are also a number of historical plays, most of them performed at outdoor sites where the dramas really took place centuries ago – such as at Moster and Kinn.

Museums are treasures of history which belong to every one of us. Whatever your special area of interest, you're likely to find a museum to your liking in Fjord Norway – from fine folk museums to public art galleries up and down the coast, museums of archaeology and natural history, fisheries and war museums – even museums on leprosy, the hydropower industry and petroleum. They're too numerous to list without doing injustice to those not mentioned.

The Petroleum Museum in Stavanger.

Whale skeleton, the Museum of Natural History in Bergen.

A *historical play about Olav the Holy is per-*
formed every summer on the island of Herøy.

No need to tell children to enjoy themselves at the
Sunnfjord Museum near Førde!

Norwegian Cuisine

Top: Fresh cod is best served with roe and liver!

Above: Traditional Norwegian crispbread, "svele" (a raised pancake) and "lefse", which come in many varieties. Delicious with sour cream and fresh jam!

One of the great pleasures of being a chef in western Norway, if only for your family, is the world class ingredients! The agriculture here is one of the purest and cleanest in the world.

Most livestock graze outside for a better part of the year. As a result, the animals are lean and trim, and their natural diet includes herbs that imbue the meat with a fine flavour. No hormones are allowed in Norwegian livestock, nor in imported meat – to the great dismay of the American beef industry. Fish farming, too, gets a clean bill of health; there has been a 99% reduction in the use of antibiotics in recent years.

His compatriots may have been the only ones who weren't surprised when Norwegian chef Bent Stiansen won Bocuse d'Or in 1993. This is the culinary equivalent of World Champion. This recognition, and the ingredients themselves, have inspired many Norwegian men and women to renewed efforts in their kitchens.

The traditional dishes of Fjord Norway generally don't complicate matters with fancy sauces or exotic herbs. Often the only seasoning added to fish, for instance, is salt. Meats and fish are often accompanied by simple vegetables – cooked carrots, mashes rutabagas or a simple cucumber salad.

Preservation is a key quality of Norwegian food traditions. Our predecessors had to store sizeable food stocks in order to survive the winter, or when they set sail for distant shores. Both fish and meat were dried, salted or smoked.

Since the potato was introduced in the 18th century, it has been a staple of Norwegian life. Some preachers saw it as virtually a religious duty to spread the good news of this nourishing root. Potato dumplings, called "raspeballer" or "komler", often accompany salted meats and are served with mashed rutabagas.

Wolffish and monkfish are wonderful new additions to the modern seafood menu. One of the easiest ways for a Norwegian to prepare a feast is to purchase several kilos of freshly caught shrimp, crusty white bread, mayonnaise and lemon – and tell the guests to bring wine and beer. A guaranteed success!

One the most famous – or infamous - Norwegian dishes is "lutefisk", dried cod which has been soaked in potash lye. There are many ways to serve it – with mustard sauce, goat cheese, or bacon and fat, or mashed split peas.

An increasing number of young chefs have no qualms about adding unexpected spices to time-honoured ingredients, or blending tradition with influences from distant countries and cultures.

It's no wonder that some travel guides suggest that tourists on a budget make do with one meal a day; a full Norwegian breakfast can make the continental croissant with jam seem like prison food. You are likely to feast on a magnificent buffet which includes half a dozen different kinds of pickled herring, smoked salmon and spiced mackerel, meats and cheeses, various jams with a selection of crispbreads and rolls, as well as sundry hot dishes. And the number of well-filled napkins which have found their way into the rucksacks of grateful backpackers is proof that breakfast really is the most important meal of the day.

More then one Norwegian housewife has been aghast when foreign guests try to cut her cheese with a knife, totally ignorant about the function of the cheese slicer lying in plain view. On the other hand, you can always point out to a Norwegian that the fork only became common in their country around 1850. Goat cheese and Jarlsberg are the most popular cheeses. If you want to live dangerously for a bite or two, you can try the rather pungent "gamalost" (old cheese).

Few nations have a higher per capita coffee consumption than Norway. It is no exaggeration that the coffee break is almost tantamount to a sacred ritual. At many offices, the switchboard won't disturb anyone during a coffee break unless the building is on fire.

Of course some ingredients don't require any preparation at all, only a refined hand to mouth movement. Small Norwegian wild blueberries are far tastier than their oversized cultivated American cousins. If they don't all end up in your mouth immediately, you can enjoy them with sugar and cream and share them with friends.

Have your knife handy to enjoy cured meat and sausages, washed down with home-brewed beer.